PINK MINK IN A SINK

To my wife and partner Cris, who encourages me to take risks and try silly things

Special thanks to Kari Martindale (editor, creative partner, friend) & Michael Carlos (best fink EVER)

No part of this publication may be reproduced, stored in a retrieval system, or transmitted in any form or by any means, electronic, mechanical, photocopying, recording, or otherwise, without written permission of the creator, except in the case of brief quotations embodied in critical reviews and certain other noncommercial uses permitted by copyright law. For information regarding permission, write to Karilogue, 2211 Urbana Pike, Ijamsville, MD 21754.

This edition: ISBN-13 978-0-9994504-9-9

Text and illustrations copyright © 2018 Aaron Parrott. All rights reserved. All photos in this work are open source and labeled for unlimited reuse.

There's a pink mink.

A mink, that is pink.

Just think!

But *why* is the pink mink pink?

Did he get into some ink?

Or was it something the pink mink decided to drink?

This pink mink is in my sink.

My sink!

It made me blink!

A pink mink,
sitting in my sink?

How will the pink mink get out of the sink?

Did the fink put the pink mink in the sink with a naughty wink?

We have to catch the pink mink sink fink!

And when we do, we'll put him in the clink!

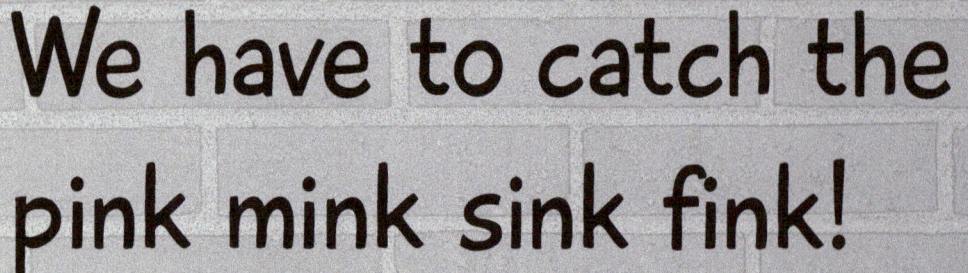

What's this?
Pink mink!
You're out of the sink!

...I'm glad you're not a pink HIPPOPOTAMUS!

www.ingramcontent.com/pod-product-compliance
Lightning Source LLC
Chambersburg PA
CBHW061932290426
44113CB00024B/2886